D0470785

What Animals Eat

HERBIVORES

James Benefield

Heinemann
LIBRARY

Chicago, Illinois

Edited by James Benefield and Amanda Robbins
Designed by Richard Parker
Picture research by Svetlana Zhurkin
Production by Helen McCreath
Originated by Capstone Global Library Ltd
Printed and bound in China by Leo Paper Group

18 17 16 15 14
10 9 8 7 6 5 4 3 2 1

Library of Congress Cataloging-in-Publication Data
Benefield, James, author.
  Herbivores / James Benefield.
    pages cm.—(What animals eat)
Includes bibliographical references and index.
  ISBN 978-1-4846-0848-7 (hb)—ISBN 978-1-4846-0852-4 (pb)—ISBN 978-1-4846-0860-9 (ebook) 1.
Herbivores—Juvenile literature. 2. Animals—Food—Juvenile literature. I. Title.

  QL756.5.B443 2015
  591.5′4—dc23   2014013681

This book has been officially leveled by using the F&P Text Level Gradient™ Leveling System.

Acknowledgments
We would like to thank the following for permission to reproduce photographs: Getty Images:
Manoj Shah, 12; iStockphotos: ElsvanderGun, 6; Shutterstock: Andrea Izzotti, 9, 23 (claws), Bestweb,
cover, Dmitry Maslov, 7, fresie12 (pine cone), back cover, 23, guentermanaus, 20, howamo, 13, Hurst
Photo, 4, Jan S., 8, Jose Angel Astor Rocha, 10, Kamonrat, 14, Mohamed Zain, 11, 23 (thorn), Olesia
Sarycheva, 16, 23 (grain), Pavel K (footprints), throughout, Peter Betts, 18, Raquel Pedrosa, 19, Rich
Carey, 15, 23 (seagrass), Serg64, 5, Vlue (roots), back cover, 23, Willi Schmitz, 17; USDA: ARS/Keith
Weller, 21

Every effort has been made to contact copyright holders of material reproduced in this book. Any
omissions will be rectified in subsequent printings if notice is given to the publisher.

007180LEOS15

Contents

Some words are shown in bold, **like this**.
You can find them in the glossary on page 23.

What Do Animals Eat?

You need to eat the right food to live and grow. Animals need the right food, too. Different animals eat different things.

Herbivores eat plants. Carnivores eat meat.
Omnivores eat both meat and plants.

What Is a Herbivore?

Herbivores get their food from plants. Like you, they can eat fruits, vegetables, nuts, and **grains**. For example, some lemurs love to eat fruit.

Some herbivores eat parts of plants that we don't usually eat. Squirrels eat tree bark and parts of **pinecones**.

How Do Herbivores Get Food?

An orangutan's long arms help it to get food. An orangutan uses its arms to swing between trees and reach for fruit.

Some herbivores find food in the ground.
Wombats have sharp **claws**. These claws help
them dig through soil to find **roots** to eat.

How Do Herbivores Eat Food?

Look at this horse's teeth. Many herbivores have teeth like this. Their front teeth cut up plants. Their back teeth grind plants into tiny pieces.

Some plants are hard to get at. The giraffe's long tongue can reach leaves from between sharp **thorns**.

Are Herbivores Predators or Prey?

Animals that hunt herbivores are called predators. Animals that are hunted are called prey. Which animal is the predator in this picture?

Herbivores need to spot predators. Many herbivores, such as this deer, have eyes on the sides of their heads. They can see all around.

Herbivores All Around

You can also find herbivores in the air. Blue and yellow macaw parrots eat foods such as seeds and fruits.

There are lots of herbivores in the sea.
For example, a green sea turtle eats seaweed
and **seagrasses**.

Can You Find a Herbivore in Your Home?

There are some herbivores we keep as pets. We can keep birds such as parrots or parakeets. Their food includes seeds.

Rabbits are herbivores, and we can keep them as pets, too. They love to eat lettuce and vegetable scraps.

Herbivores in Danger

When humans build things, they might cut down plants and trees. This happens in the Amazon rain forest. Herbivores need these plants and trees for food.

We can help herbivores in the wild by planting new trees. We can also keep some herbivores in zoos to keep them safe. For example, we can feed them the right food in zoos.

Dangerous Herbivores!

Herbivores don't kill animals to eat, but they can still be dangerous. If a group of African buffalo ran over you, you could become as flat as a pancake!

Cows are herbivores. Cows can be scared of dogs running around and might chase you and your dog. Always keep your dog on a lead if there are cows around.

True or False?

1. We call the animals that hunt herbivores their prey.

2. We eat all of the same fruits and vegetables that herbivores eat.

3. Some herbivores are in danger because humans are cutting down trees in forests.

4. We do not keep any herbivores as pets.

5. You can find herbivores on the land and in the sea, but not in the air.

6. Herbivores have grinding teeth. These teeth break down the food they eat.

Picture Glossary

claw
hard, pointy, and curvy end to an animal's finger or toe

grain
kind of seed, such as a grain of rice

pinecone
fruit of a pine tree. Seeds of the pine tree are inside pinecones.

root
part of a plant. It is usually below ground. It sucks up water and nutrients from the soil.

seagrass
like normal grass, but it lives in the sea

thorn
sharp and spiky part of some plants

Find Out More

Books

Kalman, Bobbie. *How Do Living Things Find Food?*
     (Introducing Living Things). New York: Crabtree, 2011.
Nunn, Daniel. *Food* (Why Living Things Need).
     Chicago: Heinemann Library, 2012.

Internet sites

Facthound offers a safe, fun way to find Internet sites related to this book.
All of the sites on Facthound have been researched by our staff.

Here's all you do:

Visit www.facthound.com

Type in this code: 9781484608487

Index